LITTLE CUP OF ROMANCE

LITTLE CUP OF ROMANCE

Prof. Sri Aishwarya Balu

PAPER TOWNS
PUBLISHERS

PAPER TOWNS
PUBLISHERS

First published by
Papertowns Publishers
72, Vishwanath Dham Colony,
Niwaru Road, Jhotwara,
Jaipur, 302012

Little Cup of Romance

ISBN Print Book - 978-93-91228-29-3

Cover Design by Aditi Shah
Instagram Id: @the.book.story
aditicshah01@gmail.com

He himself, litted pillar of my loving say.

Oh Darling! I'm only far away by the land,
not by our soul

We are in each other's hand for the fortune land.

"We are the little bits of each time byte."

Let our weights be weighed on this weighing era.

Let's stay as one, to be there for one another.

He is the soccer of my silence whom all
I wished to voice out -the big day.

She is the tag of my first nap
And final kick.

Spilling love over the spooning life.

You are the rare species that I wanna discover
in my soul, day after day.

You are the rhythm that I wanna inhale
in all aspects of my entire life.

Relaxed in his glamour
Switches his pathway of eradication.

One click can define our chronology.

You are the laws of all my flaws.

You are the pile of my lifestyle that never ever fades.

Be there at everytime as for everything.

You are my first fall
And the last truth.

You are the sonnet of my each eye-filled
expressions of mine, only mine.

You are the touch of my every description -
FIRST and LAST pillow sayings.

Your wings are where my rings are supposed to be.

She gathers the lost herself
To share the feelings with ourselves.

Nothing is too tight for the right-receptacle.

We both are pre-titled titled for an opened envelope.

I'm fainted for a paint in an unknown sight
for our known Art-the gallery of our life.

Limitless voyage,
Never ending love,
Unfailing Mercy".

You are the one who I'm longing for always
in all-ways my dear belonging.

Spare is rare until the right choice is done at the right moment.

I'm just alive in your breath, breathing
In which you make me complete forever.

You are just killing one of my sights
With a thousand number of your insights

Turned her lip
For his Tip-The very tip of their life

Oh, How sweet can your sugar lips magnify my glory.

Oh!!! babe,
We are twisted to tale
We are rusted to nail
We are nailed to mail
And we are mailed to rail together forever".

I'm just rusted over the dust in the dark
Until I met you the light shadow of my hallway.

His blurring vision on her flame
With a blushing insight of them.

You are the mighty poles in which
my profound galaxy beats on and on".

She is the one only one who lits the fire
on my testimonial.

She loved my imperfections
To merge out a perfect triangle.

"You are the energy wave in which
my tea-Bag is filled up".

We are loved with a love of more over each other
And not with hate of regret under each other.

He asked herself not to slave on anyone
But to outbrave on everyone.

We both are Mailed in someone's
chronicle every day.

We are the springs that profounds
in many offsprings".

It's better to reject than to eject.

We both are born to rail in someone's nail.

Let's Turn up To Tune over.

The older we get to be
The wiser we yet to be.

Be Apart
To be a part of each other.

Discouraged Thoughts
With an Encouraging spirit
Sounds pleasant.

His Inspiration
Her outcome.

One to oneself

Life is winged for Each other,
Like a hierarchical plateau-my dear friends
And there made the decision to be apart,
Either by heart nor in soul of oneselves
And it's not too far to be worried out the gate
Where it's all decided for a purpose on baggage
For Nothing But,.........
To kiss over challenges of one's army,
In which God has ordained for them
And neither the storm nor the wind,
Can never ever stop the God's plan was
Finally! It was all they wish to be,
With a cheer spot in Hot date
Marks over the pathway of Destiny.

Around! Round the Sense on her humour
Peeped herself into his flame.

Striken

Shutdown!!!
I can hear,
The mourn of world
As they Distress
Slowly over the nations
I can hear
The fear of world
As they tempted
Stumbling over the flesh
But can't get
Your spirit of faith
Why???

Fine Brookins
Outcast the Maligner.

Wind indicates the direction
But blow indicates the reason.

Don't tell the world,
You are weak
You are the spirit of godliness,
And no more the flesh of human
You are the thunder of hope,
In a presence filled lightning
You are flashes of every storm,
That Waves so curiously throughout your droplets
You are the stars around the galaxy,
That burns the darkness of all the ashes
And you are the end in the beginning of each new day.
You are the mighty hands of all phase,
Into known and unknown droplets
And you are beauty in the most profound island.

Her Eye-balls
His firewalls.

You are all that I wish to be rest of my life with.

Feel your feelings
More than your sayings.

I'll never be blinked to fill-up nothing
Until you are with me, my everything.

Every love has its own charm
And enough space to fill their own - let.

All in one say without a second choice.

Pens are just documented to ink
You're more than that.

Get together
For another decade.

Go Hard
For a ride.

No more text,
No more call,
No more hangouts,
But still alive.

True Love is like a wind,
Blows up the mind of you and me
Directs us on the path of esteemed pasture.

Holdback,
Erodes an illusion, cliffs on the coast
No more Pull-ups, just cling on the push-ups
and there where knocks the gateway of unbeaten.

(MEANING:
Dear young couples the holdback is painful
the situations look either dry or wet,
but the end is fruitful
stay thoughless ....)

Audacious she

She is the one who Believes in her spirit,
Well, still observing calmness of the nature
Delights her the fantasy Ride-in the Trait,
tributes her away from the patches,
Blown away from the period of Timidity
Overlapping with One Another on madness.

Catchy Souls

Where is his flaw?
In her perfection
How much her nectar?
Until his suck of honeycomb
How long does he prevails?
Till her very depth of wrinkles
From where he grooms?
Around her wisdom wall.

Navigation

Where is an ocean?
In the depth of her top-secret voyage
Uh, alarms out whispery waves over the chosen faith,
Fleshes out the seamanship within a hope-filled ethos.

Two-Edges

Life is winged for each other,
Like a Hierarchical plateau my dear friends
They made the decision to be apart,
Either by heart or by soul
And it's not too far to be worried,
It's all decided for a Purpose
For nothing but....,
To kiss over the challenges of army,
In which God has ordained for them
And neither the storm nor the wind can't block,
What God planned for their life
Finally! It was all as they wished to be over,
With a cheers spot in the mid of hot date
Marks over the destiny spot.

Fit-In

Busy Eye - Balls,
Stark with Naked Arrows
Strives out! Out -Bumps In,
The perfect warrior.

Mirror First sight of one's love

She is the one who Believes in her spirit,
Where the goodness bestowed on each other
There pleases the soul -in shines out to peace,
Well, observing calmness of the point
Delights her, Rides in the fantasy vehicle
Uh, overlapping with one another dwells
Out the reflection in an unknown wizardry.

Deliverance In- Distress Out

Hard at it, where she Missed him
There Hustles out! For the betterment of life
Haven't Twisted on a Narrow Elegant -cut,
Bumps away, a little notes of Musical Arrow
Steadfast the emotions of faith over Trust
Oh!!!
What a Magical shot? Indeed in the knees of one's knees,
Kicks off, the perfect fear of evil
Calls upon the spirit of Holiness of conversation
Whispering out The holy words of wine,
"For Nothing shall be Impossible with God our lord ".
And finally, filled her the deliverance of joy.

Knock your Courage

She is Not the girl used to be
Nor the women that she had imagined
She would Grownup to wisdom out
BRICKS OUT HERE AND THERE!

Certainly, Not as together as she expected
But somehow more stuffed - in
Than she would never be imagined.

Frequently, Engages her the own spirit-
spirit of holiness
As much towards the pull of forced gravity
Outribes her a softness of lamp.
She was softer from all the storms
And not as far as season of wait in nearby
Finally, she was completely unapologetic
In all of her Tarnished glory.

Stolen

Heart like a soul,
Beat like a Mate,
Anchors the spirits over fleshy bones.

Proposal

His Sparks
Her glitters.

Meaning:

(The Moment he sparks, glitters her soul
Spreads out the bliss, The enlightenment
With an Erased Darkness on Marked glory)
-New year

Alarm -IT

Thoughts are Mystery
Until we wake up.

Peep-Out

Be a TravelGram
In a viber called Devices.

Conversation

Oh!!! Babeee
We are Salted to Pepper,
We are one to oneself,
We are Alpha to omega,
We are Blink to Think,
We are Dusted to Dare,
We are Mixture to Texture,
We are Solid to liquid,
We are spicy to Honey,
We are Milk to chocolate,
We are bless to bliss,
We are wine to Mine,
We are wound to Bound,
We are Armour to Humour,
We are colo to Rumm,
We are Dimple to wrinkle,
We are wrinkle Twinkle

Coins

Two phases,
Two Direction,
Either Courage Or a Discourage,
Decides the challenger on shot.

Antibiotic

The one which preserves
The one which Fight
The one which Resists
The one which Anticipates
The one which Relives
The one which put an end to
So.....,
I'm alive,
I'm strong,
I will stand Bold,
I'm more than mood /swinger,
I will never stop praying for,
I'll move forward,
Because He is my antibiotic.

An Opened view by him

hmmm, why do we fear silence?
We stumble for the weak in the darkness
Awkard in the insight of fire- test
Rearranging the stuff of negatives assets
With an exploring attitude of Negative pull-in/outs
Nowadays, As we Are Afraid of Hello
And we are of the Good -Byes
Freaks, freaking out the enough off explosion on society
To say "MORE PREVENTION! LESS CYNICISM"
Isn't it?
It's also a cause of greatness and would suffice on.

Thinking Matters

Are you in the lockdown Boiler?
Yup....
Hmm, it's okie.... But
Where is the chiller?
Lol, Hehe....
Ah! Temperature Matters
Aren't They?
Hmmm, yep. That's Great.

White-Out

Oooohhh,
It's a Day like the Mist
A night like a Harshy the fuzz,
Makes the shuttered -Doorway.

Candy

Sweetness in her lips
Outcomes on his charms
Delights the Nourishment of the souls.

Puzzled

Sequence of alphabets,
Arranged in numbers,
Enrolls the logistics.

An overnight Kick

Among the sleepless night,
There calls upon the mind into grave
Into the silence of unsaid feelings
And the heart gets struck over there
Suddenly, Knocked the doorway of galaxies
As the moon kisses over the stars of infinite souls
With a kick in his good time
Bliss in her soul appeals the sweetest heavenly joy
Makes over a Romantic Bowl...

Meaning: (Frozen In her own galaxy)

Our journey with her

April 2,
A lovely Meet in a place where it all started,
One glance at her that makes my heart beats faster
The more harder we explain the strategy of voyage,
Transmitting convince over the vow, slowly bestows the honour of our relationship
Let her tears creep out of joy, and pride filled her soul.
Makes out a perfect fit-In triangle.

SUNKISSES

All along the desert,
It's quite a misty look of his charms
Twisted her glory of glaring sunshine,
Spells her with words of thirst over and over
Appeals there a majesty on magical cloud view
With a spectrum of feelings like a colourful rainbow
Delighted overwhelmed the gracious Wine.

Anchor

To him, she was direction
To her, He was shape
Together, they made an anchor.

A Nap in his kin
Says rib in the vein.

Love -Eyes full of love

A walk in the clouds on the nature of her sight
Stumbled my feet away, away from the darkness
Around a Milky Way glaciers of pathways
As he speaks in drifts voice, voicing out
Baby girl, you deserve a cloud nine walk-in
I'm so, so sorry.....
This what love was supposed to feel like
But baby girl, every time you hurt, I hurt ....
I Love Him.

Togetherness

Bliss! Bliss! Bliss!
Day like a Heart,
Night like a Beat,
Together they made the whole day.

Feel your feelings

Uh,
Can you hear them?
The flap of a manuscript and fence
Hmm, Yeah flip - flops the thoughts
Filled with secret puzzles
Drifted onto the spectrum of feelings.

Unknown Destiny

Thinking literally, where you can't move on
Moving probably, where you can't think on
Moulding firmly, where you can't stand on
But standing still, where you can mould on

(Be still, know that God will fight your battles)

Enlightenment

On a Dusky valley with a soul-filled meet,
Across the stormless blowing wind of summer
As he knocks into veins by converting fear into faith,
Her soul rages over transferring of the negativity
into positivity
And there Relishes the soul.

Are you in darken clouds?
Let courage be your Hallway,
Let faith be your Masterpiece,
Let positivity be your footprints,
Let destiny be your vibe station,
And let success be at your Doorstep.

Are you an overnight owl?
Or a crested cuckoo on the walls of mystery
Absorbing the warm & coldness of nature,
Glaring in the castle of love for romance.

Eternity

Arms around the waist
Until her wrinkles

1) Off the shore
There lies hope.

2) Blink on
Bliss over.

3) Choose passion over pride
Success over failure.

4) Kickoff the shore
To enlighten the best in you.

Psychology of Balance

Are you riding a bicycle,
Or a motor rider on the slope - pathway
Riding out the season of passion
in Breathtaking Airway,
Thinking over and over upon rotation of metaphors
Glaring the sense of conviction in two-headed
arrow space.

Dream Challengers

A man behind her vision
A woman with his mission
Into the collaboration of sacrifices and waves
Pins up their Knots.

Composition of Life

Trucks in the personality, warms up the light of heat
In a vintage assest, creates the vision of life,
With a rhythm of mission into keylines of them,
Paves our a path switch in the silence of ocean,
Breathing all over and over with an unknown silence,
Rashes over the flesh of human spirit,
And finally, the Humanity sucks.

Emotions

It's well to be there
But it's not all right to be always there
Therefore, observe how deep the pain it had been
For nothing, but for the purpose of burying a suture
And to be Born again with the spirit
Not thy within the flesh.

PRE-Address

When you feel the cup is unoccupied,
Be sure that it overwhelms with goodness
Neither supply nor to borrow the season of favour,
To shuttle off your loneliness into toxicity
Well, spaced out the pastures entire lifetime,
On the pathway of eminent gesture.

1) His loyalty
Her fragrance.

2) Beauty in her flaws
Overflows The cup.

Roses over the thorns,
Rises the glory of mist clouds,
Walks in the kingdom of heaven,
Scorches away the perfect fear.

Mess in the pause

Oh, it's twisted above the storms of skytop,
And wintered under the darkness of clouds
Ragged and calmed the nuisance of pollution,
As it swarms in a cyclic gap of oceanography
On the most awaited island the peace.

One-Striped Arrow

The day where I looked into your eyes full of love
Swiped away feet, the very feat of my five fingers
Opened the valves, the way towards galaxy of bliss
Slowly, drifted away the Thirstyness of my soul
Within a heart bloomed vessel of mine
In your vein.

Perfect Hitch

Out for a night,
Not for a date,
But for love at first sight.

Waves

Thoughts over the night,
Feel under the soul,
Tides everywhere around the spirit.

Holy wine
Thy tasted the couplets of Romance.

To him, she was the creech
To her, he was the bleach
Together they met at the beach.

Acknowledgement

This fiction part is dedicated to my father in person who is the well known educationist ,principal of the government higher education and also known as state level resource person (Author of educational books) of the state level PTA association.

"His wildest woe for me on that day is my successive bow on this day" –heir of educationalist".

And also to the Anchor of my soul - successive traveller of this perfect voyage.

About the Author

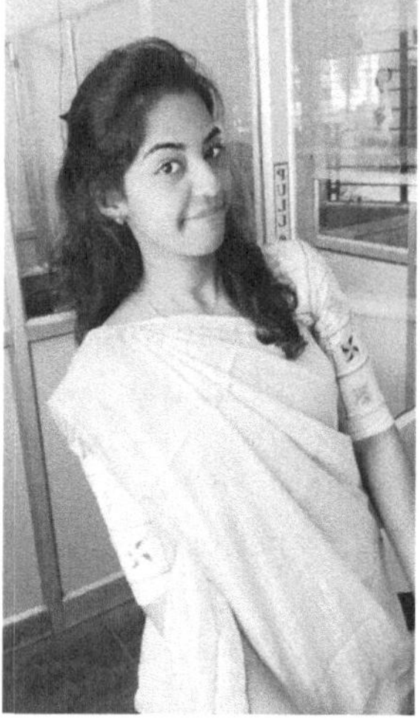

AISHWARYA BALU is a 24 year old woman from the TOP-NOTCH sector on the southern region of Tamilnadu. She is an amusing personality charged with a sea of love. She is a former Software Engineer and in 2019 was the English professor of a private engineering college. And also handling up the core and management related paper with a placement award by ANNA University.

She obtained a bachelor degree for engineering in the field of IT from ANNA UNIVERSITY BOARD. And also received out her full time ride scholarship on government college for her MBA (HR) COURSE. Anchoring was her major throwback moment in her college life at many international conferences. Journalism plays out the major thirst right from her childhood days, where she used to write out most relevant scripts for many schools and profiled universities at various national and international conferences.

She is the one who loves to convert thoughts into words from this how passion carried herself through her. According to her, "love is the weakest substance in the hardest battle found in the courageous attitude of one to oneself in this challenge filling world".

It's a great part to have you all here (my readers) bounded like a milky -way galaxy turn over the sky. Let's Enjoy the fundamental ride of the earth on the footpath of love and Romance.